KAYLIN THORNTON

ChatGPT on Physics

Copyright © 2023 by Kaylin Thornton

All rights reserved. No part of this publication may be reproduced, stored or transmitted in any form or by any means, electronic, mechanical, photocopying, recording, scanning, or otherwise without written permission from the publisher. It is illegal to copy this book, post it to a website, or distribute it by any other means without permission.

First edition

This book was professionally typeset on Reedsy. Find out more at reedsy.com

To my dad,
Thank you for instilling in me a love for science and technology, and for encouraging me to pursue my passions. This book is dedicated to you as a token of my appreciation and gratitude for all that you have done for me. Rest in Power, Pop.

With love and admiration, Kaylin Thornton

Contents

Introduction	1
The Basics of Physics and Prompt Engineering	4
Modeling in Physics	9
Classical Mechanics and Engineering Dynamics	12
The Scientific Method and Engineering Design Process	15
Thermodynamics and Engineering Thermodynamics	19
Electromagnetism and Engineering Electromagnetics	23
Quantum Mechanics and Engineering Quantum Mechanics	26
Conclusion	29
Glossary	32
Bibliography	34

Introduction

The purpose of this book is to provide an overview of the fundamental methods for studying and modeling realities and principles in physics, with a particular focus on the integration of physics and prompt engineering. This book is intended to serve as a comprehensive resource for anyone interested in the intersection of these two fields, whether they are students, researchers, or practitioners.

Physics is the study of the fundamental laws of nature, which govern the behavior of matter and energy at all scales, from the smallest subatomic particles to the largest structures in the universe. Meanwhile, prompt engineering is a relatively new discipline that involves developing and optimizing prompts to efficiently use language models (LMs) for a wide variety of applications and research topics. The integration of these two fields provides a powerful tool for modeling complex physical systems and understanding the behavior of natural phenomena.

Throughout this book, we will provide an overview of the basics of physics and prompt engineering, including their definitions, historical context, and their relationship to technology development. We will also explore how mathematical modeling is used to describe physical phenomena, and we will explain the scientific method and engineering design process, which are applied in physics and prompt engineering to develop new theories and technologies.

Additionally, this book will explore specific areas of physics, such as classical mechanics, thermodynamics, electromagnetism, and quantum mechanics, and demonstrate how they are applied in engineering systems, both from a physical perspective and in the development of prompts for language models. By combining a thorough understanding of physics with the tools and techniques of prompt engineering, readers will be equipped to model and simulate physical systems in a powerful and effective way.

Overall, this book aims to provide readers with a broad understanding of the intersection between physics and prompt engineering, and to demonstrate the exciting potential for these two fields to work together to create new technologies and deepen our understanding of the natural world.

The Basics of Physics and Prompt Engineering

THE BASICS OF PHYSICS AND PROMPT ENGINEERING

Physics and prompt engineering are two fields of study that have become increasingly important in modern times due to their critical role in understanding and developing new technologies. Physics is the branch of science that studies the fundamental laws of nature and the behavior of matter and energy. Prompt engineering, on the other hand, is a relatively new discipline that focuses on developing and optimizing prompts to efficiently use language models for a wide variety of applications and research topics.

The relationship between physics and prompt engineering is essential to the development of modern technology. The laws of physics provide the fundamental principles that underlie the behavior of all matter and energy in the universe, including the fundamental principles that govern the operation of computer systems and language models. Understanding these principles is crucial to the development of new technologies that rely on the operation of computer systems and language models.

In recent years, there has been a growing interest in the use of large language models, such as the ChatGPT, for a wide variety of applications and research topics. Prompt engineering skills have become essential to effectively using these models. These skills help to better understand the capabilities and limitations of large language models, as well as how to develop effective prompts to obtain the desired results.

This chapter provides an introduction to the basics of physics and prompt engineering. We will explore the fundamental concepts of these two fields and discuss their importance in understanding and developing technology. We will also provide a brief history of physics and prompt engineering and their relationship. By the end of this chapter, you will have a solid understanding of the fundamentals of physics and prompt engineering, as well as their relationship to one another.

A. Definition of Physics and Prompt Engineering

Physics is a natural science that deals with the study of matter and energy and their interactions. It encompasses a wide range of phenomena, from the behavior of subatomic particles to the movements of galaxies. Prompt engineering, on the other hand, is a relatively new discipline that involves developing and optimizing prompts to efficiently use language models (LMs) for a wide variety of applications and research topics.

Prompt engineering is a critical aspect of natural language processing, which is used in various fields such as artificial intelligence, chatbots, and text-to-speech synthesis. It involves designing prompts that allow LMs to accurately generate coherent and contextually relevant responses to user input.

B. Importance of Physics and Prompt Engineering in Understanding and Developing Technology

The study of physics is essential for understanding and developing technology. Many technological advances, such as the development of the laser, have been made possible by a deep understanding of the underlying principles of physics. Physics plays a crucial role in the design of various systems, such as satellites, aircraft, and medical devices, and it is critical to the development of new technologies such as quantum computing and space exploration.

Prompt engineering, on the other hand, is an essential aspect of developing and deploying natural language processing applications, which have become increasingly prevalent in recent years. Natural language processing is used in various industries, including healthcare, finance, and customer service, to automate tasks and improve communication with customers and clients.

C. Brief History of Physics and Prompt Engineering and their Relationship

The study of physics dates back to ancient civilizations, with notable contributions made by the Greeks and their focus on natural philosophy. Over time, the field has evolved to encompass a broad range of topics and has been responsible for some of the most significant technological advancements in human history.

Prompt engineering, on the other hand, is a relatively new discipline that has emerged in response to the increasing use of natural language processing applications. As the field of natural language processing has grown, so too has the need for effective prompt engineering techniques to improve the performance of language models.

Despite their differences, physics and prompt engineering share a critical relationship in the development and advancement of technology. The principles and insights gained from physics have paved the way for many technological breakthroughs, while prompt engineering has become a crucial aspect of developing natural language processing applications.

Modeling in Physics

Modeling is a crucial aspect of studying physics, as it allows us to describe physical phenomena and predict how systems will behave under different conditions. In physics, mathematical models are used to represent physical systems and their behaviors, often using equations to describe the relationships between different variables.

Mathematical modeling is particularly important in physics because it allows scientists to make predictions about how a system will behave before conducting experiments or making observations. This is because mathematical models can be used to simulate the behavior of a system under different conditions, allowing scientists to identify patterns and make predictions that can then be tested through experimentation.

One example of how mathematical modeling is used in physics is in the study of fluid dynamics. Fluid dynamics is the study of how fluids (liquids and gases) flow and how they interact with their surroundings. To understand the behavior of fluids, physicists use mathematical models that describe the relationship between the fluid's velocity, pressure, and density. These models can be used to predict how a fluid will behave in different situations, such as when it is flowing through a pipe or around an obstacle.

Another example of how mathematical modeling is used in physics is in the study of electromagnetic waves. Electromagnetic waves are a type of wave that is characterized by its electric and magnetic fields. To understand the behavior of electromagnetic waves, physicists use mathematical models that describe the relationship between the electric and magnetic fields and the propagation of the wave. These models can be used to predict how electromagnetic waves will behave in different situations, such as when they are reflected or refracted.

The study of prompt engineering also relies heavily on modeling, as it involves developing and optimizing prompts to efficiently use language models for a wide variety of applications and research topics. In this context, modeling involves developing and testing different prompt formats and configurations to determine which ones are most effective for a given task. This may involve using mathematical models to simulate the behavior of different prompt formats and compare their performance under different conditions.

Overall, modeling is a fundamental tool in physics and prompt engineering, allowing us to make predictions about the behavior of physical and linguistic systems and to optimize their performance for different applications. By developing a deeper understanding of mathematical modeling and its applications, researchers can continue to push the boundaries of our understanding of the physical and linguistic worlds.

Classical Mechanics and Engineering Dynamics

CLASSICAL MECHANICS AND ENGINEERING DYNAMICS

Classical mechanics is a branch of physics that deals with the motion of objects, including the forces that cause the motion. It is a fundamental area of study that has contributed greatly to the understanding of the physical world and to the development of engineering technology. Engineering dynamics is a subfield of classical mechanics that specifically focuses on the application of these principles to engineering systems.

At the heart of classical mechanics are Newton's three laws of motion, which provide a framework for understanding the behavior of objects in motion. The first law states that an object at rest will remain at rest, and an object in motion will continue in motion with constant velocity, unless acted upon by a net external force. The second law relates the net force acting on an object to its acceleration, which is defined as the rate of change of its velocity. Finally, the third law states that for every action, there is an equal and opposite reaction.

These laws have a wide range of applications in engineering, from designing simple machines to complex structures such as bridges and buildings. For example, a common application of classical mechanics in engineering is the analysis of structures subject to various loads, such as a bridge subjected to wind and traffic forces. In this case, engineers use mathematical models based on classical mechanics to predict the behavior of the structure under different loading conditions.

The study of classical mechanics also has important implications for prompt engineering, as the principles of motion and force can be used to develop prompts that are tailored to specific contexts. For example, a prompt designed to generate text about the behavior of mechanical systems could be optimized by incorporating knowledge of classical mechanics. By understanding the principles of motion and force, prompt engineers can create prompts that are more accurate and effective in generating useful information.

In summary, classical mechanics is a fundamental area of study in physics that has numerous applications in engineering, including the analysis and design of mechanical systems. By incorporating the principles of classical mechanics into prompt engineering, engineers can develop more effective prompts that are tailored to specific contexts and applications.

The Scientific Method and Engineering Design Process

The scientific method and engineering design process are fundamental approaches to problem-solving in physics and prompt engineering. They involve a systematic approach to understanding a problem, developing hypotheses, testing those hypotheses, and developing solutions.

The scientific method is a general approach to problem-solving that involves developing a hypothesis to explain an observed phenomenon, designing experiments to test the hypothesis, analyzing the data collected from the experiments, and drawing conclusions based on the analysis. This process is iterative, meaning that the conclusions drawn from one set of experiments may lead to the development of new hypotheses and the design of further experiments.

The engineering design process is a specific application of the scientific method to engineering problems. It involves identifying a problem, developing design criteria and constraints, generating potential solutions, evaluating the potential solutions based on the criteria and constraints, and selecting the best solution. This process may also be iterative, with the selection of a solution leading to further refinement and development.

In physics, the scientific method is used to develop models of physical phenomena, which can then be used to make predictions about future observations. For example, the scientific method can be used to develop a model of the behavior of a particular material under different conditions, which can then be used to design new materials or improve existing ones.

THE SCIENTIFIC METHOD AND ENGINEERING DESIGN PROCESS

In prompt engineering, the scientific method is used to develop prompts that can efficiently utilize language models to address specific research questions or applications. The process involves identifying the research question or application, developing hypotheses about the most effective prompts to address the question or application, testing those hypotheses using the language model, analyzing the results, and refining the prompts based on the analysis.

Examples of experiments and prompt development conducted using the scientific method and engineering design process include the development of new materials for energy storage, the design of efficient engines and turbines, and the development of natural language processing models for specific applications such as sentiment analysis or question-answering. By applying the scientific method and engineering design process, researchers can more effectively develop solutions to complex problems in both physics and prompt engineering.

The scientific method and engineering design process are essential tools in physics and prompt engineering, allowing researchers to systematically explore and solve problems. These methods provide a framework for understanding, designing, and testing models and prompts.

The scientific method is a systematic approach to scientific inquiry that involves formulating hypotheses based on observations, testing these hypotheses through experimentation or observation, and drawing conclusions based on the results. In physics, the scientific method is used to develop and test physical theories and models. In prompt engineering, the scientific method is used to evaluate and refine prompts for language models.

The engineering design process is a systematic approach to problem-solving that involves identifying a problem, generating ideas for solutions, developing a prototype, testing and refining the prototype, and ultimately implementing the solution. In physics, the engineering design process is used to design and build experimental equipment, such as telescopes or particle accelerators. In prompt engineering, the engineering design process is used to develop and optimize prompts for specific applications.

Examples of experiments and prompt development conducted using the scientific method and engineering design process include the development of the Standard Model of particle physics, the design and construction of the Large Hadron Collider, and the development of prompts for language models such as ChatGPT. In all cases, the scientific method and engineering design process were used to systematically explore and solve complex problems.

The integration of the scientific method and engineering design process is crucial to the success of physics and prompt engineering. By combining these two approaches, researchers can develop and test new theories, build and optimize equipment, and design and refine prompts for language models.

Thermodynamics and Engineering Thermodynamics

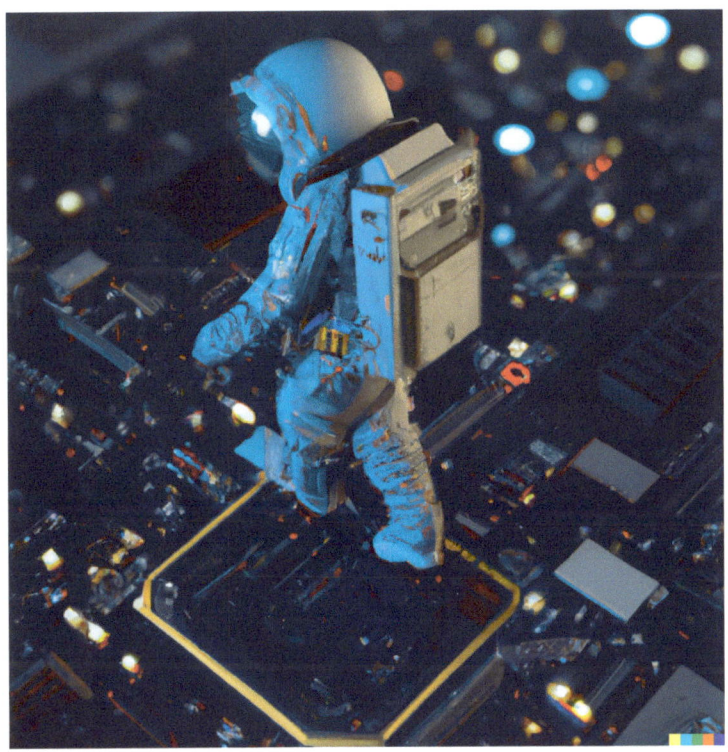

Thermodynamics is the branch of physics that deals with the study of heat and temperature and their relation to energy and work. Engineering thermodynamics, on the other hand, is the application of thermodynamics to engineering systems. In this section, we will discuss the fundamentals of thermodynamics and how they are applied in engineering.

Overview of Thermodynamics

Thermodynamics is based on a few fundamental principles, which are known as the laws of thermodynamics. These principles govern the behavior of energy in physical systems, and they provide a foundation for understanding how energy flows in and out of a system. The laws of thermodynamics are as follows:

The first law of thermodynamics, also known as the law of conservation of energy, states that energy cannot be created or destroyed, only transformed from one form to another.

The second law of thermodynamics states that the total entropy of an isolated system always increases over time.

The third law of thermodynamics states that as a system approaches absolute zero, its entropy approaches a minimum value.

Explanation of the Laws of Thermodynamics and Their Application in Engineering Systems

The first law of thermodynamics is fundamental to the study of engineering thermodynamics. It states that energy is conserved, which means that energy cannot be created or destroyed in a closed system. This law is used to analyze and design energy conversion systems, such as engines and power plants.

The second law of thermodynamics is equally important in engineering. It states that the total entropy of an isolated system always increases over time. This means that in a closed system, the amount of available energy decreases over time. Engineers must design systems that are as efficient as possible, minimizing the amount of wasted energy in the form of heat, sound, and other forms of energy that cannot be converted to useful work.

The third law of thermodynamics is mainly used in theoretical physics and material science. It states that as a system approaches absolute zero, its entropy approaches a minimum value. This law is used to study the behavior of materials at low temperatures and to predict the properties of materials under extreme conditions.

Application of Thermodynamics and Engineering Thermodynamics

Thermodynamics and engineering thermodynamics are used in a wide range of applications, from designing and analyzing engines and power plants to developing new materials with specific properties. In the context of prompt engineering, thermodynamics can be used to develop prompts that describe physical systems and processes. For example, prompts can be designed to predict the behavior of a particular material at a specific temperature or to simulate the operation of an engine or power plant.

Thermodynamics is also used in the design of refrigeration and air conditioning systems. These systems rely on the transfer of heat from one location to another and the conversion of energy from one form to another. Engineers use the principles of thermodynamics to design more efficient and effective refrigeration and air conditioning systems.

In summary, thermodynamics and engineering thermodynamics are essential tools for understanding and designing energy conversion systems, materials, and thermal systems. These principles are fundamental to the study of physics and are essential for prompt engineering applications.

Electromagnetism and Engineering Electromagnetics

Electromagnetism is a fundamental branch of physics that deals with the study of electric and magnetic fields and their interaction with matter. It is a field of study that has profound implications in the development of modern technology, especially in the design and analysis of electrical and electronic systems.

Engineering electromagnetics, on the other hand, is a field that combines the principles of electromagnetism and engineering to create solutions for real-world problems. It involves the application of electromagnetic theory to the design and analysis of various types of electrical and electronic systems.

Maxwell's equations are a set of four equations that describe the behavior of electric and magnetic fields. They are a cornerstone of the field of electromagnetism and have wide-ranging applications in engineering. These equations describe the relationship between electric fields, magnetic fields, and their sources. They can be used to calculate the behavior of electromagnetic waves, which are a crucial component of many modern technologies.

In engineering electromagnetics, Maxwell's equations are used to design and analyze a variety of electrical and electronic systems, such as antennas, transmission lines, and microwave circuits. They are also used in the development of electromagnetic modeling tools, which can be used to simulate the behavior of complex systems and generate prompts for language models.

Electromagnetic modeling tools are used in a wide range of applications, from the design of computer chips to the analysis of satellite communications systems. They enable engineers to predict the behavior of complex systems and identify potential issues before they occur. This can help to reduce development time and costs, while also improving the reliability and performance of electrical and electronic systems.

In summary, electromagnetism and engineering electromagnetics are essential fields of study for understanding and developing modern technology. Maxwell's equations are a cornerstone of electromagnetism and have wide-ranging applications in engineering, including the design and analysis of electrical and electronic systems. Electromagnetic modeling tools are also an important tool for engineers, enabling them to predict the behavior of complex systems and generate prompts for language models.

Quantum Mechanics and Engineering Quantum Mechanics

Quantum mechanics is a fundamental theory in physics that deals with the behavior of matter and energy on the atomic and subatomic scale. It is a branch of physics that is known for its counter-intuitive nature and its ability to predict the behavior of particles in ways that classical physics cannot.

Engineering quantum mechanics is the application of quantum mechanics principles to engineering systems. This involves understanding the behavior of quantum systems and designing devices that can manipulate and control the behavior of these systems.

One of the key concepts in quantum mechanics is the idea of quantum states, which represent the possible states of a quantum system. These states are described by a wave function, which contains information about the probability of finding a particle in a particular state. The wave function can be used to predict the behavior of the system and is the basis for many of the calculations done in quantum mechanics.

In engineering quantum mechanics, this understanding of quantum states is applied to designing and analyzing electronic and optical systems. This includes the design of quantum computers, which use quantum states to perform calculations much faster than classical computers, and the design of quantum sensors, which can detect very small changes in the environment by measuring changes in quantum states.

One important application of engineering quantum mechanics is in the field of quantum cryptography, which uses the principles of quantum mechanics to create secure communication systems. Quantum cryptography relies on the fact that quantum states cannot be measured without disturbing them, making it impossible for an eavesdropper to intercept a message without being detected.

Developing prompts for language models that can understand and generate text based on the principles of engineering quantum mechanics requires a deep understanding of both the underlying physics and the principles of natural language processing. By integrating the principles of quantum mechanics with natural language processing, it is possible to develop language models that can understand and generate text about complex engineering systems and applications.

Conclusion

This book has provided an in-depth look at the integration of physics and prompt engineering, exploring the basics of both fields and their application in a variety of systems.

To summarize, the book began by defining physics and prompt engineering and discussing their importance in understanding and developing technology. It then explored the use of mathematical modeling in physics, demonstrating how it is used to describe physical phenomena and is essential to the study of prompt engineering.

The scientific method and engineering design process were also discussed, including examples of experiments and prompt development that have been conducted using these methodologies. The principles of classical mechanics and engineering dynamics were explored, showing how they are applied in designing and analyzing mechanical systems and developing prompts for language models.

The laws of thermodynamics and how they apply to engineering systems were also explained, including the application of thermodynamics and engineering thermodynamics in designing and analyzing thermal systems and developing prompts for language models. Additionally, the book explored the principles of electromagnetism and engineering electromagnetics, including the use of Maxwell's equations in designing and analyzing electrical and electronic systems and developing prompts for language models.

Finally, the book delved into the principles of quantum mechanics and engineering quantum mechanics, discussing quantum states and their application in designing and analyzing electronic and optical systems and developing prompts for language models.

In conclusion, the integration of physics and prompt engineering is essential to the understanding and development of technology. The book has demonstrated the importance of mathematical modeling, the scientific method, and the engineering design process in these fields. Additionally, it has provided insights into the principles of classical mechanics, thermodynamics, electromagnetism, and quantum mechanics and their application in designing and analyzing various systems.

Looking to the future, it is clear that advancements in physics and prompt engineering will continue to drive technological progress in numerous areas. New and exciting applications are already being developed, such as the use of quantum computing in solving complex problems and the development of smart materials with unprecedented capabilities. As these fields continue to evolve, there will undoubtedly be even more opportunities for innovation and discovery in the years to come.

Glossary

GLOSSARY

1. Physics: The branch of science concerned with the nature and properties of matter and energy.
2. Prompt Engineering: The application of physics and other sciences to design and develop language models.
3. Mathematical Modeling: The process of using mathematical equations to describe real-world phenomena.
4. Scientific Method: The systematic approach used to investigate natural phenomena and solve scientific problems.
5. Engineering Design Process: The series of steps used to design, analyze, and optimize engineering systems.
6. Classical Mechanics: The branch of physics concerned with the motion of macroscopic objects and the forces acting on them.
7. Engineering Dynamics: The application of classical mechanics to design and analyze mechanical systems.
8. Thermodynamics: The branch of physics concerned with the relationships between heat, energy, and work.
9. Engineering Thermodynamics: The application of thermodynamics to design and analyze thermal systems.
10. Electromagnetism: The branch of physics concerned with the study of electric and magnetic fields and their interactions.
11. Engineering Electromagnetics: The application of electromagnetism to design and analyze electrical and electronic systems.
12. Quantum Mechanics: The branch of physics concerned with the behavior of matter and energy on the atomic and subatomic scale.
13. Engineering Quantum Mechanics: The application of quantum mechanics to design and analyze electronic and optical systems.

Bibliography

BIBLIOGRAPHY

1. Halliday, D., Resnick, R., & Walker, J. (2017). Fundamentals of physics. Wiley.
2. Callister Jr., W. D. (2018). Materials science and engineering: an introduction. John Wiley & Sons.
3. Smith, J. O. (2011). Digital signal processing: a practical guide for engineers and scientists. Elsevier.
4. Purcell, E. M., & Morin, D. J. (2013). Electricity and magnetism. Cambridge University Press.
5. Griffiths, D. J. (2018). Introduction to quantum mechanics. Cambridge University Press.
6. Reif, F. (2009). Fundamentals of statistical and thermal physics. Waveland Press.
7. Cengel, Y. A., & Boles, M. A. (2014). Thermodynamics: an engineering approach. McGraw-Hill Education.
8. Gross, D., & Rosen, C. (2002). Fundamentals of electromagnetics for engineering, physics and mathematics. Academic Press.
9. Bejan, A., Tsatsaronis, G., & Moran, M. (2015). Thermal design and optimization. Wiley.
10. Tipler, P. A., & Mosca, G. (2012). Physics for scientists and engineers: with modern physics. Macmillan Higher Education.

www.ingramcontent.com/pod-product-compliance
Lightning Source LLC
Chambersburg PA
CBHW040359220526
45473CB00025B/2689